Accelerant

Bill Yarrow

Nixes Mate Books
Allston, Massachusetts

Copyright © 2019 Bill Yarrow

Book design by d'Entremont
Cover photograph by Lauren Leja

All rights reserved. This book or any portion thereof may not be reproduced or used in any manner whatsoever without the express written permission of the publisher except for the use of brief quotations in a book review or scholarly journal.

ISBN 978-1-949279-09-2

Nixes Mate Books
POBox 1179
Allston, MA 02134
nixesmate.pub/books

for Leah

Contents

The City Rises in Me	1
The Point	3
Sin Curve	5
I Alone Am Escaped	6
Eli in the Middle of the Night	7
Sin Embargo	8
Flame Thrower	9
Visiting Our Slab	10
Life with Fish	11
Pinochle In My Snout	12
Swords	13
Taking Off the Knives	15
The Learning Curve	16
The Whole Debt	17
Meet the Beatles	19
Artefact	20
A Pack of Matches	21
Satan and the Moon	23
Machete	24
Not a Villanelle	25

Language Out of Water	26
Lobbying for Compromise	27
Emptiness and Absence	28
Turbulence	29
In Time of the Breaking of Congratulations	30
Magnum Otis	31
Yuletide Cranshaw	32
Theorizing Salsa	34
Sacrifices of Famished Promise Made to Apology	35
Neural Tones	36
Body Parts	37
Poeta sin Brazos	40
Pruning	42
Poet between Oxnard and Van Nuys	43
Timbre	45
Less Scenery	47
Down Ballot	49
In My Hometown	50
Stendhal Nightclub	52
J'recluse !	53

Accelerant

The City Rises in Me

Cities! Cities! I have lived
in cities: habitual, arrogant
cities circumscribed by cities

on the alert for alacrity
filled with false vitality
rising revised out of history

burgeoning cities bloated
with stoic pride, notorious
for hope, filled with ethical travail.

These cities, yes, but also
cities reticent, inferential
embedded with desuetude.

A decade here, a decade there,
to what end? Position. People need
locus, not looseness, in their lives.

What's a road? A swift excuse
for a city at each end. What is
not a city? Nothing.

Socrates lived in a city.
So did Meyer Lansky. The city
rose against them. That's what

cities do; they rise,
sometimes in us,
sometimes against us.

The city rises in me.
I hear it whisper.
I ignore its roar.

The Point
for A, B, and C

I stood on the Point and rooted for the truth.
Everywhere were starfish angels, each one in my way.
The sun, like a drunken bum, stumbled across the sky.

> *If you're not any more interesting sloshed*
> *than you are sober*
> *then what's the point?*

My model was late for her sitting.
"You're like a library book – overdue!" I said.
"Then I'll take off all my clothes
like I did for you last time," she said,
"and then I'll be re-nude."

> *If you're not any more interesting frizzled*
> *than you are frozen*
> *then what's the point?*

"What's nubile with you, my dear?" I asked.
"That's highly salacious, you know" she said.
"Wasn't he the King of Ethiopia?" I queried.

> *If you're not any more interesting moist*
> *than you are torrid*
> *then what's the point?*

"You're a piece of hot pie," I said,
"crusty with the sweet and creamy center."
"But there'll be no massacre
of the General Custard this time," said she.

> *If you're not any more interesting polluted*
> *than you are pristine*
> *then what's the point?*

I stood on The Point and looked out at the sea
and imagined I saw a pod of yellow whales, but that
was just the sun pissing twilight into the distant foam.

Sin Curve

Sin? Nah. There's just kindness and hurt.
The sun kills the grass. The wind hurts
the leaves. The sea ravages the shore.
But nothing in Nature goes to Hell.
Neither is anything in Nature kind.
Kindness and cruelty are human add ons.
Everything eats everything else but only
human beings make a big deal out of it.
(The volta cometh) Maybe you need
to be a premie. Maybe you need to
grow up in Westport. Maybe tutoring
is in your future. Maybe debate.
Maybe a wife, nasty, brutish, and
short. You know, the life of Hobbes.

I Alone Am Escaped

we are running through the unguarded alley at midday
our pursuers in blue – future suicides armed with knives

if we can make it to the zocalo, perhaps we can hide
in the faded aluminum advertising kiosk

the sun beats down relentlessly like pleading
threatens to reduce us to mechanized dust

all of a sudden, we are surrounded by grasshoppers –
they jump in our hair, nest under our arms,
bang on our teeth

in the confusion, I lose my appetite for existing
kiss a tree with my skull, fall into the dark abyss

when I wake, the sky is dull cinnamon

frantic to find salvation, I limp to the deserted
escarpment only to find it overrun by toads

in my despair, I truly begin to despair
– the distance to the zocalo is still six city blocks

Eli in the Middle of the Night

I stood beneath the mountain
in a flank of malefactors.
The sun stood in the sky
like Eli in the middle of the night.

More than once. More than twice. Three times
God called to me from the thunderstorm
of good and evil, but my ears were filled with songs
of wounded birds and the howls of dying dogs.

I stood in the city, in the fields,
in the stillness of a regnant rain.
Silent among the slaughtered beasts,
I stood like Eli in the middle of the night.

Sin Embargo

I like badness. Don't all the really good
films have the word "bad" in their titles?
*The Good, the Bad, and the Ugly. Bad
Day at Black Rock. Bad Lieutenant.
Baadasssss! The Bad and the
Beautiful. The Bad Seed.*

Evil's another story, a story
whose orphan narrator is misery,
married to pain, son of suffering,
sibling of spleen. I have seen evil.
If you have too, you know there's
but one bad way to get rid of evil.

Retrieve the ragged dagger. The night
is just weak enough for insurrection.

Flame Thrower

It was 2:00 in the afternoon
on Tuesday, July 11, 1959.
I was sitting in the air-conditioned Capitol Theater
watching Gregory Peck in *Pork Chop Hill*.

The theater was empty
but looking back
how could it have been?
Why would it have been?

Wouldn't I have looked around
to see who else was there?
Maybe not. On the screen in front of me
enemy soldiers confronted flame throwers.

Flame throwers! Strapped to the backs
of soldiers. Hoses spitting flame.
I had never seen anything like them.
I couldn't turn my eyes away.

Sixty years later...
Fifty films later...
Forty wars later...

watching people burn
has lost much of its appeal

Visiting Our Slab

Watch this space: sanded, painted, and polished
like a braggart, calibrated like an artisan pipe
bomb. The future *in camera*. What goes away
can"t stay away. Neither can one Google redemption
but go ahead and try. Pretend the marshlands
aren't haunted. Pretend the buzzer won't beat
the half-court shot. Pretend happiness.
But as you gather the gorse of your longing,
as you reticulate your infantry, as on the way out you
huddle your missiles yearning to bereave,
leave us the legal recipe for the accelerant of hope.

Life with Fish

First fish are caught with ping pong balls
and taken home in plastic bags.

Second fish are sought with sticks
poked in the foam of sewage streams.

Third fish nibble beads of bread
dangled in a graveyard pond.

Fourth fish in the jetty wash
snatch small bits of thawing squid.

Fifth get hoisted, get yanked out
of proud dark photographed bays.

Sixth are hunted off resort bridges
after midnight with flashlights and arrows.

The seventh jump at your eyes
as you drag their net along the mud.

Eighth fish snap at silver flies
trailed across a rainy lake.

Then someone baits a hook for you,
but you're much too smart for that.

Pinochle in My Snout

The paneled linoleum basement rec room
with tables set up for pinochle, salami, and
schnapps. My uncles, grandfather and father
at one table; my aunts and mother at the other.
The blurry TV on. The bookcases with glass
fronts and carved locked doors holding auction
volumes and foreign coins. My three sisters
in ballerina tutus running up and down the stairs.
My unemployed younger cousins on the back lawn
smoking Luckies. My coiffed older cousins discussing
the subdivisions of the Republican future. Albums
of peeling Polaroids, dirty doilies, fuzzy rugs.
The fetching wreckage of an arsoned heart. "Does
anyone want anything else to eat? Anyone? Anyone?"

Swords

Dawn in the forest. A blue mist
rises around the legs of two men
convened to kill each other.
Crumpled on the ground are two black
capes. A winter sun shows above
a grove of whitened trees. Light
glints in raised identical blades.
The sound of directions. Two men
rush toward each other's lives.

My father is weary. He leans
back in his chair onto pillows
which support his pain. He's tired
of the walls knowing nothing, of
ignorant furniture. Why can't
his room understand he's dying?
Or his wife his fears? He closes
his eyes, dreams of this against
that. He solves his suffering.

My sister walks in on his breathing.
Not wanting to wake him, she wonders
whether to douse the image on the screen.

December. Dawn. Two men in a forest.
The Count of Sorrow. The Duke of Loss.
My perfect father, she thinks, and
bends down to kiss him. Begging to be
brandished, the tumor, like a sword,
rises from his chest toward its cruelest duel.

Taking Off the Knives

The table in me will no longer
support the fruit, throws off
its tablecloth, refuses to admit
one dish. It's outraged by the
weight of the pepper and salt.

No more vases! it cries.
No more napkin rings!
A moratorium on salad forks
and serving spoons! An ultimatum
from the parquet walnut table.

Yes, of course. No more vases.
See, see, they are taking off
the soup tureen, the artificial flowers,
the tarnished pewter and the fruit.
They are taking off the polished knives.

But where shall I take my dinner?
And where shall I entertain guests?
What use now for the round-back chairs?
The table is silent, shining, petulant
in its posture and refusal to be set.

The Learning Curve

There's always something negative to say:
that's what she's learned by listening to her
pain while exercising on the heads of

pins. In silence, she bakes zucchini bread
and reads *The Lancet* a lot. There are days
she opens the valves of her attention

to the sprawl of phlox and felicity,
but she's blind to the creeping peevishness
of stevedore philosophers. Doesn't

she understand the reactionary
pessimism of the local helots?
What she needs is a hot shot of Cedar

Rapids, a close dose of liberation
biology. Look up! Look up! She-wolves
are eyeing the somnolent underclass

while bearded Cialis bankers hawk
municipal treachery, sip Arnold
Palmers, and feed on underdone seabirds.

The Whole Debt

just as I was launching my life, extending the web of my friendships, adding magicians, librarians, architects, horticulturalists, house lawyers, horse lawyers, CIOs, videographers, EFL instructors, instructional designers...

just when the langoustines had me by the throat, when the side exits were all blocked, when the nacreous clouds began to move in, when the power grid was stretched to breaking, when the atrial gas main was poised for rupture, when the Mad River was rising, when the medallions of my palms were beginning to itch...

just when the air was loud with the sound of invisible mockery, when the world, paralyzed by littleness, was becoming dull, when all the birds headed for the bourbon hidden in the corn, when cheers of ill will resounded from the abandoned sawmill, when craven acolytes were craving ions...

just when the sky was dark with birds, the ground black with snakes, the river choked with otters, the mesa teeming with beetles, the mountains pocked with bees...

my stepparents slammed the door of the oven of the soufflé of death and the feisty yeast of conjured life began to rise.

Meet the Beatles

I was twelve years old in 1963.
The Korean War had ended ten years earlier.
WWII eight years before that.
Kristallnacht seven years before that.
Sacco and Vanzetti were electrocuted in 1927.
The Titanic sank in 1912.
In 1968, I was buying comix at head shops in New Hope.
In 1972, I was swimming at nude beaches in Big Sur.
In 1978, I was parking cars and writing eulogies.
In 1981, I was changing diapers in Rego Park.
In 1985, I was grading papers on Darwinism.
It's been fifty-two years since I was twelve years old.

Artefact

The only thing I have left
    of my maternal grandfather
        is a small hand-held mirror
            made of ivory.

It sits in the upstairs
    bedroom dresser drawer
        like an only child

I have yet
    to see myself in it.

A Pack of Matches

I.

across the way
insulated from snow
by a slim cleavage in the hills

the wet nurses gossip
to the storm clouds
about the old men in the jail

on the opposite side of the lake
inky frauds seek celebrity
as if that porousness were protection from despair

twelve floors up
I sit on used furniture
and recalibrate loss

II.

in the Tropic of Parkinson's
the heartless moon looks on in stupor
as the ocean catches frail meteors in its arms

outside the Castle of Logos
the palsied rain
conspires with tattooed thunder

around the corner
a colony of ruined trees
laments a bend in the weather

then the cheaters
ever merciless
begin losing at cards

Satan and the Moon

1.
Satan and the moon are made of cheese.
That's what my wife taught my kids.
They all dropped out of school.

2.
Don't believe what you are told. Invest
in what you can't see. If you watch TV,
watch it inordinately. Turn it off in December.

3.
Patrician vicissitudes run ransack
with benign alignments of the brain.
Never never never feed the publicans.

Machete

aspirin and Band-Aids in baggies
astronauts with flags on their swimsuits
addicts with raging colitis
none of the above

blandishment heaped upon Girl Scouts
board games invented by florists
beachcombers drunk at the drive-in
none of the above

magnets left in a chapel
manatees shunted in tunnels
mystics sedated with sulfur
none of the above

wellness empowered by ampoules
weather defended by dancers
whimsy unharnessed to outlook
none of the above

Not a Villanelle

screams in the blonde
polyp air then peroxide
nausea pushing up
ringed fingers tarpaulin
tested flesh moldy rose
perfume privileged tits
porcelain privacy surprise

porcelain privacy surprise
perfume privileged tits
tested flesh moldy rose
ringed fingers tarpaulin
nausea pushing up
polyp air then peroxide
screams in the blonde

Language Out of Water

All of speech is just like life – maddening
in its small colors and declivities of spirit
and beauty. What we need is less hysteria,
less flap. Words are words. They come out
unannounced. A slim process, hardly
mysterious. Even our teeth understand
how we speak – but not when we speak
in torsion, tongues, or brute translation.
The problem's feeling – its misery and
muteness. Not to mention knowledge,
hot, wild, which saying's helpless to abet.
Talking's a kind of commonsense angling:
language is a fish, truth – a broken net.

Lobbying for Compromise

Dip me in pollen and pour on the bees
(the steaming water turns the honey hot)

Anoint my boiling head with boiling oil
(the mind has acquaintances but no close friends)

Lead me to still waters and push me in
(to curry false favor with the gods)

Stupidity is baffling only to intelligence
(the dull *squint* when innocence bestrides surprise)

I've seen the sun set silver on a river
(and maneuver the sacred distance the battered heart eschews)

I canceled my semi-daily subscription
(the foetid paper arrives anyway)

I fall upon the thorns of poetry
(some things just can't take a hint)

Emptiness and Absence

The difference between emptiness
and absence is the difference

between happiness and vice.
Like a group text, one informs

the other. Like an ovarian cyst,
inside one is the other. But not

as a debt but as an invader,
a malevolent congregant,

snacking with false benevolence
on the confident host from within.

Turbulence

Give all to turbulence. Give all
to risk. Let the rich membrane
rip. Turn the volume of raw
squawking up. Invite riot.
Seat tumult at your table.
Punish politeness. Decorum
is a villain, moderation an assassin.
The only chance for happiness
is to excommunicate all calm.

In Time of the Breaking of Congratulations

What keeps people from asking for help?
Too often the shame of being helped. Like
my recently divorced friend Delbert Freck
who tries to deflect the pain of his severance
by repeating "May divorce be with you" to
co-workers and bar mates. Everyone laughs
but just to appease him. The coat of sarcasm
is durable but not warm, so no information,
not any of any value, is forthcoming. Rather,
he coaxes acquaintance out of friendship
and sleeps among the intoxicated rocks.
I take him aside. *Del, Del, what are you
doing? How can I help? What do you need?*
Del: "You know any women into anal beads?"

Magnum Otis

I've been married to Penny for thirty
years. I take care of my Penny and let
the dolors take care of themselves.
The other day she said to me, "Otis,
let's lose some weight." *By us, you mean
me, right? You think I've gotten fat.*
"Oh, Otis, I don't think you're fat, but
let's walk together a little more often
and a little more briskly. For our hearts."

For *our* hearts. She's so sensible. Heart
logic. My heart's a little muddy. I don't feel
quite so clearly, but concepts, on the other hand,
– those, I get. Rousseau's *amour-propre*.
Sartre's *mauvaise foi*. The human coefficient
in Leonov. The economy of suffering in Howells.
But not investing. Not stocks. Not futures. Not swaps.
Nothing generates any interest. My literal pennies,
shiny anniversaries of prudence, resist return.

Yuletide Cranshaw

I meet him at the office Christmas Party.
Otherwise our paths in life would never cross.

A drink in both red hands, stirring the placid
pot of conversation, trying to increase its
inner heat, he declaims to no one in particular,
"An ounce of whore is worth a pound of spouse!"

That's because you never married, I think.
Only a man who's never not been alone
could think a thought like that. He laughs,
pokes the upper arm of the prettiest woman
at the makeshift bar. "Right? Right?" he asks.

Most of the women shift uncomfortably
and drift away. A few who enjoy blushing
move closer. He becomes the nucleus
of a spirited group of mostly neckless men.

The oily conversation behind me flares up.
Sharp sparks from it seem to threaten the tree.

Cranshaw likes his bon mot so well he says again,
"An ounce of whore is worth a pound of spouse!"
Raucous laughter erupts. Bully cheers resound.

To a young woman of recent acquaintance
I chuckle, *Well, in* my *experience at least,
I've found that an ounce of spouse is worth
much* more *than a pound of whore.*

She stares at me with frosted disbelief.
I endure a silence reverberant as greed.

Theorizing Salsa

Janet and I
had the tilapia
fish tacos and
talked about God

God ordered the veal
cutlet and was rebuked
by the vegetarian Politburo

The beer had a divine odor which
attracted the wasps of mortuary remorse

Sacrifices of Famished Promise Made to Apology

when she says she's lonely
he hands her last week's *TV Guide*

when accidentally he steps on her hair
she accidentally misplaces his keys

once upon a time, twice upon a time
two lovers lay upon a candied beach

Neural Tones

"A rose is a rose is a rose," wrote Gertrude Stein.
I prefer Wanda LaFrond's version: "Erós is erós
is erós," she said, sitting next to me in the dark
patisserie where we were listening to a torch singer
light the gloom of our recent divorces. My divorce
was two months older than hers, but we were both
still in the infancy of our dissolutions, the infected
flecks of sour love still visible on both of our chins.
"Who's your favorite poet?" I ask her during the lull.
I'm into the vegan poet To Fu, she says. *What about you?*
"I'm heavily invested in Tao Jones, the Wall Street poet."
She tries to smile. *What do you most regret?* "Regret?
About Hora? Not being kinder to her, I guess."
Fondness is in our power; kindness is not. "I wish,
but it's the other way around," I say sadly. She puts
her hidden arms around me. I reciprocate. Look
at us, she murmurs. *Tristan and Isolde without
the adultery.* "Well, you can't have everything."
She: *No? I heard otherwise.* Then
frozen dawn waltzed into the bakery and against
all good sense, I arose and arose and arose.

Body Parts

They were playing chess with body parts of children they had sacrificed to God.

The battalions of pawns were tiny teeth. The darting rooks were eyes. The frosty knights were hollow cheeks. The blushing bishops were ears. The Queen was a nose. The King was a tongue, upright but unsteady like a vertical snake.

Antoine was red, his soldiers bristling and bloody. Emily had black, her men dark with decay.

Antoine went first and moved the tooth in front of his tongue one space forward. Emily moved her same tooth forward two squares.

Antoine took out his nose's cheek. Emily nudged her tooth further forward.

Antoine matched her by moving out his other cheek. Emily considered his move and put her hand on her ear.

Antoine attempted the moves leading to Blake's Mate, but as he went through those tired motions, Emily had moved out all of her black teeth, forming a moat of absence between her front and rear lines, her nose proudly exposed.

Then Antoine played the Irresistible Tongue. Emily countered with the Insatiable Eye.

It was as if they were playing two different games or playing two different kinds of chess, one landed, one lunar.

I gave up my space in the front row and pushed out through the thronging crowd which howled or moaned at each succeeding move.

The hall was air conditioned and, as I was cold, this spurred the urge to empty my bladder.

"Who's ahead in points?" I asked the bearded man in the urinal next to mine. "No pieces have yet been exchanged," he said, zombielike, staring straight in front of him.

I zipped up and washed my hands.

I would have liked to have stayed, but having given up my seat and realizing there was no viable way back into the hall, I left, regretful but resigned.

I read in the next day's paper that patriarchy, though threatened, had prevailed. Antoine had won, but, so shaken had he been when playing Emily, he ceded the championship title to her.

Emily thanked him but declined the offer. She refused to win the crown by forfeit and was applauded in the press for her integrity.

"Self righteous!!!" cried her fans.

"Self righteous!" cried her foes.

I was undecided. I could understand both reactions as I could see both aspects of the game, its divergent opponents and contradictory styles.

Ultimately though, it made no difference.

The government stepped in and, citing sanitation and health concerns, banned all games played with body parts.

Poeta sin Brazos

"yo, poeta sin brazos, perdido
entre la multitud que vomita"
— *Federico Garcia Lorca*

I knelt by the knee wall
painting with black magic marker
gross defects in the hardwood

my mind overflowing
with flooding lines from Lorca
and the lithe piano rites of Mose Allison.

This was not the first time
I had been to the Emerald Necklace
in springtime

the red moss
tattooing the bank
like an incision filled with sand

I would visit the Priority Triangle
later that afternoon and buy my wife
a Marla harness just in case.

How she loved it when at the Buttery
in our youth I quoted Yeats to her:
"I will arise and come now."

Then, I was Villon the beloved
rogue, Horne Tooke the shuttle
cock, Cowper the shoe horn.

"It's time for lunch," said my lean
assistant Izquierda. "Hungry?"
Very! How does Vietnamese sound?

She nodded vigorously. And thus
I came to escort my fey duende
to the outskirts of Pho King.

Pruning

in the orchard
below the mountain
rain was falling

geese flew west from the lake
like prayers
ascending to clouds

dead branches lay in aisles of apple trees
dead twigs
feathers from dead birds

the world was silent as a psalm
but there were rifles
to protect us from the calm

Poet between Oxnard and Van Nuys

The butter of summer was melting onto
the toast of the town, a town which I had
visited only in dreams, dreams I had failed
to remember despite earnest attempts
to recall their evocative details, details
so reverberant they made the old men
outside the café sob with happiness
for their outmoded childhoods among
the tangled brambles and dry rivers
as they remembered soft rendezvous with lovers
long lost to futures unclouded by intrigue.

It was the summer of mutton, the summer of
jellyfish and jacaranda. The gypsy caterpillars,
had commandeered the lobby of the fortress.
One rolling hill reconsidered its profile
and decided to light out for fiery Iowa.
Sunlamps flashed off and on in a Morse code
of bitter inconsequence. Dilations of happy
mockery, indices of jocular boxes, tropes
of moroseness, modular degeneration and
fascist neuralgia – the preternatural detritus
of opulence leading to no end but one – optimism.

A universe of pearls, a multiverse of swine.
Cultivated fields of alternating texture.
There is no privilege in description, but neither
is there license in horizon. What of the solitary
bougainvillea—not in molly, not even in bloom.
But what harm can six beers do before noon?
What bad can happen in a stand of trees?
Who dare interrupt the symmetry of tilled
hills or planted vines? "It's getting foggy,"
said the man beneath the incarnadine hat.
But the inviolet sun had other ideas.

To the music of fronds cascading from blonde trees,
the beach, decked in swim vestments, preoccupied
by scorpion waves, retreated from boxer crabs corralled
by rat-hair orphans wearing ill-fitting Jasper hats
and I thought, the only thing continuous is time.
How strange to look out at waves from a train. How
odd for sand dunes to roll past the eye. How otherworldly
to have train tracks parallel the dolphin road. Unsettling
to see the landscape ripple and crest and churn.
I had gone north looking for rescue. I found it sitting
in a rental train looking out at the passenger coast.

Timbre

under a circle of blatant maples
an old man sits watching two plush
cyclists rush the borders of the university
in search of incautious rendezvous

of course no one reads about
tradespeople anymore or looks
in the commonplace for
exemplars for everyone's
under a different shade, but
consciousness is still delight
and while living remains difficult
it's not officially backbreaking

statistically there are now more
butterflies in the world than
there are moths, that is to say
more mouths at the spigot
than assembled at fluorescence
but what beautiful fences
keep us at arm's length from
danger, at hair's breadth from seraphim

*I want a foolproof pudding
but the only porridge I can
find is full of sticks
and bitter liquor*

a broken sun drips maroon
pollution onto the screen
of things as time records
a tan girl wearing an "I am
a Spartan" t-shirt; meanwhile
the last Athenian contemplates
himself in graduate statuary
and stained bas-relief urinals

we will not live to see much change
but one day some indulgence will
be born whose short thought and
sharp alarm will recondition mercy

– and that will change everything

Less Scenery

I.

    one mountain has a dedicated cross

opposite, the hill is dotted with hospital haciendas
ringed by avocado trees

    over there's the empty mesa

a power plant abuts an arroyo
its parking lot designed to be invisible to cows

the roofs of Starbucks call out for Dunkin' Donuts

watch out for the pornographic   railyards
watch out for seduced   beauty

accommodation parks, industrial hotels, financial
eateries, car apartments – what hasn't been yet created?

the sun starts raining through the clouds
the horizon shifts seats on the train

    welcome to the House of Insufficiency!

II.

come, put your arms around my grief
assuage with your breasts the boils on my heart
massage with your tears the fecund desert of my eyes

but the world is too variegated
the landscape too too narratable
I need fewer scenarios

      less scenery
more home
      more depot
not more Home Depot

but the invincible
refuge
of

        nativity

where mirrors are not the petty kings
where prestige is not the frothing queen
where the only thing to eat

is not the lushness of empty space

Down Ballot

SHE votes
>based on hair type

HE lives off the largesse
>of women with slim hips

SHE works from nine to three
>for a cosmetic dentist

HE spends his afternoons
>wandering the Zuma hills

SHE developed shin splints
>from running after her children

HE can't get over his triumphant puberty
>in New Rochelle

HER new man will have a Yale lock
>on his conscience

SHE will train him to be the cashier
>at her church

HIS childhood barber is running for office
>in Milwaukee

HE would contribute
>but the down ballot is never a sure thing

In My Hometown

in my hometown pinhead Joe
plays mumbly-peg
with a sharpened spoon

in my hometown manila
is the flavor and cul de sac
is the address

in my hometown the Catholic girls
know all the words
to "Louie, Louie"

in my hometown the post office
serves Doritos
and lime beer

in my hometown yellow
Ford Falcons
people Old York Road

in my hometown
all the crosses on the mountain
are upside down

in my hometown
the Thalidomide baby
just turned sweet sixteen

Stendhal Nightclub

soon enough

the orphans will unsheathe
their pistols and the hash fields
will be emptied of sparrows

soon enough

the cobras will unhinge
their jawbones and the pampas
will be lonely for muskrats

soon enough

the microbes will unlock
their cell walls and the bloodstream
will be noisy with forfeit

not soon enough

J'recluse !

The diagnosis? A lesion. *Of
enthusiasm*, Fitzgerald said.
*The sallow wing of the shadow
of madness,* according to Baudelaire.
For Nijinsky: *Love*, aka *God*.
For Groddeck, *It*. That's all *it*.

What do you call it, you, who look
at me with impossible eyes, you, who
call to me ineffably from the fog, you,
irredeemably Braille, who run toward
the many savagely ravaged by rage,
who, seeing hope's aloneness, caress,
who despite death's best intention,
– for there's NO alternative – persist?

Acknowledgments

"A Pack of Matches" *(Skidrow Penthouse)*
"Artefact" *(HCE Review)*
"Body Parts" *(Ginosko Literary Journal)*
"Down Ballot" *(MadHat)*
"Eli in the Middle of the Night" *(Iodine Poetry Journal)*
"Emptiness and Absence" *(Punch Drunk Press)*
"Flame Thrower" *(Sententia)*
"I Alone Am Escaped" (Blue Fifth Review)
"In My Hometown" *(PoetsArtists)*
"In the Time of Breaking of Congratulations" *(Red Fez)*
"J'Recluse" *(Literary Orphans)*
"Language Out of Water" *(Peacock Journal)*
"Less Scenery" *(Home Planet News Online)*
"Life with Fish" *(The Literary Review)*
"Lobbying for Compromise" *(The Packingtown Review)*
"Machete" *(Festival Writer)*
"Meet the Beatles" *(Otoliths)*
"Neural Tones" *(Nixes Mate Review)*
"Not a Villanelle" (Literary Orphans)
"Poet between Oxnard and Van Nuys" *(Olentangy Review)*
"Poeta sin Brazos" *(Home Planet News Online)*
"Pruning" *(Hayotzer)*

"Sacrifices of Famished Promise Made to Apology" *(Red Fez)*
"Satan and the Moon" *(Used Furniture Review)*
"Sin Curve" *(Alephi)*
"Sin Embargo" *(Unlikely Stories)*
"Stendhal Nightclub" *(Festival Writer under the title "Dog-Eared Sparkplug")*
"Swords" *(Hayotzer)*
"Taking Off the Knives" *(Poem)*
"The City Rises in Me!" *(Staxtes)*
"The Learning Curve" *(blossombones)*
"The Point" *(Unlikely Stories)*
"The Whole Debt" *(Home Planet News Online)*
"Theorizing Salsa" *(Pank)*
"Timbre" *(Alephi)*
"Turbulence" *(Deer Heart)*
"Visiting Our Slab" *(Mojave River Review)*
"Yuletide Cranshaw" *(poetic diversity)*
"Flame Thrower" and "Pinochle in My Snout" also appeared in *Incompetent Translations and Inept Haiku (Červená Barva Press)*.
"Not a Villanelle", "Satan and the Moon," and "Theorizing Salsa" also appeared in *The Lice of Christ (MadHat Press)*.
"The Learning Curve" also appeared in Wrench *(erbacce press)*.

About the Author

Bill Yarrow, Professor of English at Joliet Junior College and an editor at the online journal *Blue Fifth Review*, is the author of *Against Prompts*, *The Vig of Love*, *Blasphemer*, *Pointed Sentences*, and five chapbooks, most recently *We All Saw It Coming*. His work also appears in the anthologies *Aeolian Harp*, *This is Poetry: The Midwest Poets,* and *Beginnings: How 14 Poets Got Their Start*. He has been widely published in both national and international journals and has been nominated eight times for a Pushcart Prize.

42° 19' 47.9" N   70° 56' 43.9" W

Nixes Mate is a navigational hazard in Boston Harbor used during the colonial period to gibbet and hang pirates and mutineers.

Nixes Mate Books features small-batch artisanal literature, created by writers who use all 26 letters of the alphabet and then some, honing their craft the time-honored way: one line at a time.

nixesmate.pub/books

www.ingramcontent.com/pod-product-compliance
Lightning Source LLC
Chambersburg PA
CBHW052105110526
44591CB00013B/2353